Third Body

Third Body

Michel Delville

Translated by
Gian Lombardo

Quale Press

This book was translated and published with the generous support of the Communauté française de Belgique.

This book was originally published in Belgium as *Le troisième corps* © 2004 Michel Delville and éditions Le Fram.

Cover: "Front View of Thorax" from *Gray's Anatomy, Descriptive and Surgical,* circa 1862.

ISBN: 978-0-9792999-7-1 trade paperback edition

LCCN: 2009925832

Quale Press
www.quale.com

Contents

For Gilbert, Germain and Vincent

Therefore there's a Third Body. But it only achieves unity
in our consciousness since you can only know it
by having it sundered and smashed into bits.
—Paul Valéry

Third Body

Where you come to terms with the crush of whatever steps between, bumps into and stumbles among the vestiges of words, with the liberated thinking of those who do not claim a monopoly on free thought, with the spilling of the latter into dream's uninhibited language, with virtual crimes committed in a state of most obvious doubt, with providential victories of the flesh against the spirit weakened by the confusion of consciousness's doctrines, with opposites that do not cancel each other, with the sub-realistic layout of the ligne claire *that encloses the colors of Walloon life, with the lamest and most premeditated jokes, with theorists and philosophers of highest order who speak more for the sake of speaking than to actually say something.*

Pulling the strings

of the loop universe, whose ends only meet ends. Hidden world where unseen bonds inject form and function into the twin consciousnesses of beings and things. Unstable misapprehension of men and women blindly desiring what will be, plumbing depths, their faces contorted as they await an unmistakable apparition. Appreciate the state of excitation of bits and particles. Apprehend depictions of everything that's been believed. Everything happens as if there were some force of calm, obvious stubbornness that thwarts any separation factor by its very structure.

rise in sudden flips, slips, slides, enmeshed pulses. Some consume others. Seize your pound of flesh and scram. In a flash. After that, expect eternity to age. Then slowly. One thought draped in the customary call to autophagous vesperal mastication, vociferating the most pungent deconstructive propositions. And then — supreme infamy — delicately wiping the edges of its lips like a proper young woman.

When the thirteenth

fragment masters the other half of the world. Orifices sullied by the anguish of the primal scream of too much emptiness. Guided by the assignments and rote mechanics of an education ruled by the cries and injunctions of chronic frustration, of intrinsically undignified transitional objects, of what's neither placed within nor without.

Story of a Presence

The eye doesn't see beyond sky. What remains is only a gesture, a palm waving. You already begin to think of something else. An itch rears its head, weak at first and not very well defined. Soon, it becomes more tenacious and insistent until it is impossible to fight, like trying to ignore the heated and troubling voices that seem to issue from somewhere else and whose twisted echoes gently reach you before getting tangled in the damp dark. Initial fears gone, you conclude by seizing it, by caressing it to better domesticate it, by understanding that its source, even though it's unknown, is lost in an incomplete effort that carries the signs of "our insuppressible hope." You even surprise yourself predicting the limits and contours of its countless divagations and airs.

On Friendship Between the Sexes

Some scruples and guilty inflections stir up certain oblique tics thirsting for brio and scandal. There follows a curious blend of suspiciously excessive happiness gazing at the center of a furious and unrecognizable silence. In the end, provisional goodbyes, so knowingly ungainly.

After all, you tell yourself that it's not so serious. Everyone has the right to seek a receptacle in proportion to their desire — indeed, to withdraw from any feeling of obligation with regard to him or her whose availability bears the sign of incipient complicity without requiring anything in return. Thus, our sensitivity to disordered and inaccessible things must be based, in a way altogether rather natural, on a form of guilty consensus.

because conversation will always constitute an inferior art. We speak about things without bothering to consider them as objects. We forget to examine the image that reflects our deeds and our statements.

Besides, we are trying to discover the minor defect that yields sadness and sickness. Beneath an attitude of indifference seep the remnants of a changing and fleeting rancor, a morbid fascination for everything that refers to others' confusion, as well as for the slightest weakness and betrayal of men and women of good or bad intent.

In those moments, what comes to the soul is the equivalent of a wave crossing the surface of a puddle of muddy water. Without visible cause, the undulations occur suddenly more distinctly and frequently, the turbulence weaker and more isolated. Surprised and naïve, you see then the consummate dejection of those bent on eluding their shame of emptiness. Admittedly, no punishment, no entreaty can breach this obsession. You can conquer this illusion only by distinguishing the murmur of the spirit from that of lips.

We Embrace Each Other by Name

Montaigne envisioned "an inexplicable and fatal force," as mediator of our union: "We were looking for each other before we found each other, and through what we heard of each other, which caused a greater effect on our affections than the reason of the reports may bear, I believe by some heavenly order."

But we

spoke these words more than once. Too many of them striving for the goal of serving a very modest cause. From now on a spirit not so much ironic as tragicomic and whose main function is to bar passage of dissatisfied moods that engage our sense of isolation.

Now, you tell us, it's time to keep watch over the indeterminate mob of men and women who no longer sleep. It's time to give up all that deprives us of everything. Ultimately with the suspect virtue of keeping silent to avoid destruction.

You still tell me that the rules of this game were made up thousands of years ago.

However, each

of our affections questions the relation between thought and thing. For him, cutting a scene is a kind of latent nostalgia. It always ends up imposing its gesticulatory sequence, its slivers of solidified narration. You reason, close your eyes in vain, staring at space. Nothing doing there. It is as if it were always too late. Embarrassment grays and dries. There reigns here a mystery pregnant with a mysterious abundance, even more distressing than the dead shadows that come to lean against the window, eagerly tightening around the neck, legs swinging as if isolated from the void in which they move, guanotizing the air with their lymphatic punctuality. It invades the atmosphere and claims what is owed him. You try to dispel it with a wan smile that wisdom believes best to destroy.

For some embarrassing situations

the first impression is one of duration and rhythm. They take considerable time to develop before they reach their more extreme and improbable limits. You can, for example, fearfully dream of a balcony crammed with naked bodies, filthy and restless, whose touch would become an embrace, whose embrace would become threats, up to needless confusion. With hair standing on end, with terrified eyes that, at daybreak, contemplate a jawbone that fell and broke in the bath-tub and where you try to fish out its shattered pieces using tiny hooked spoons encrusted with cheap zircon.

Some recommend

a gradual dissolution whose stages would correspond to those that did nothing more for us, in the end, than render us alone, without granting us at least the consolation of being unique. So much time, so many diffuse tremors, color of splenetic abyss.

Interruption, intentional

and systematic of physical functions and pangs of conscience. Suspension of congestions of the diaphragm clouded by the call of the belly open like a wound seen from the inside (not an intimate room, but a common dormitory overwhelmed by too harsh a light). Decay of the soul by the subterfuge of the fear that attracts contrary poles and creates the spark that will suffice to bankrupt rhetorical and protoplasmic excesses of the infamous celibates of the spirit.

To hell with these suicidal embraces, this pasty and grandiloquent pathos, this moaning sensuality that trepans skulls, breaks hearts and distends bodies! From now on we need calm. We need something new and distinctive. Need matter, too, fibrous and premature, malleable and robust, light and fulgurating. Matter from which to adorn our merry bellies with an exquisite exoskeleton that would invite more than one vagrant soul to rejoin its own body.

Because, in the end, my poor friend, you must testify — EVERYONE witnesses a tragic and sordid epoch!

The Great Return of the Flesh

Breathing becomes slow, veins stir, fists clench. Yet everything seems to be happening normally. Objects couple in a lazy collapse, in wise but brutal pairs. With an almost extraordinary tranquility, they stir up everything by their passage. It's as if they wanted to show us evidence of their latest shared disappointment — a discrete and sibylline mood crouched in the heart of some dusty couch.

The woman exudes approachability, a worthy and severe opulence.

The man seems most favorably disposed.

Coda: Reciprocity of Elective Sympathy in a State of Repressed Hilarity

One single, unique body filled with saliva and sweat, dream and moistness, ready to explode in your face. From the depths of a pair of withered and wheezing lungs, it sputters clouds of transformed moisture whose practical value can be described as an irregular series of gifts, a paradoxical system that restores exuberance to falsehood and demands contempt achieved by the shift toward luxury.

[Sung:] *There, all is merely benevolence and voluble cordiality anchored in substance. Mutual agreement reigning in the act of dazzling others. Ordered and irreversible dispersion of states of meaning in becoming.*

A hymn

to the quiet pregnant virgin shadow lurking at the edges of the
wet dream of a heretic wretched Carmelite nun and so welcome
sprinkling the ground with wave after wave of fleshy secretions
an eye that weeps for the loss of that primordial element up to
judgment day safe in a sleep for which all hope

> *she whom he would take*
> *in his arms tenderly*
> *where his love would give her*
> *thus united as one*
> *with the father would lead her*
> *unto the same pleasure*
> *which God enjoys she would enjoy*

(John of the Cross)

Hearths

stilled by the cry of flesh that always says yes will manifest a sin-
gular certainty, growing increasingly stronger as our desire for
freedom grows, which in a troubled soul — in its most abstruse
proposals — the need not to fake relief from cruel and criminal
mental continence from day one militates against the hope of
going beyond the confines of the self.

An arm

thrust to undo what links us to the earth the shoulders and the
look that weighs down arms that curve in and unencumbered
hands

Suddenly everything

seems enveloped in an inexplicable beauty, heavy and humid as the air that surrounds us. An atmosphere conducive to the collective contemplation of wrong objects whose zany deceptions furnish an inexhaustible supply of amusement and atonement.

IV

You readily

admit that
fascism is very much the synthesis
of mysticism and bestialism
— *i.e.*, the paradoxical coincidence
of pleasure and inhibition —
but you are more reticent
to consider the consequences
of recent transformations
of the everyday sensation
of *fear* into an egalitarian
speech, civilized and
resolutely modern, on
economic and social
relationships

But social thought

is frequently at
the heart of our most
urgent concerns — it
provides us an alibi where
confusion babies the
vilest and most shameful
sentiments

when the nightmare of entropy
watches us
in a fit of temper where
any intended or accidental
discharge
results in a loss of energy
when any act of sexual intercourse connects
to a suicide
when an afflux of blood disperses these thoughts
finally
despite all attempts to maintain
the harmony of tender bodily
extremities with their surrounding objects

when these moments
occur
we would want to learn how to
consent to our own end
that's neither in the world
nor out of the world

V

Violence to Meat

Masked bloodstained withered skin, tongue reddened by an impudent Parisian accent, chomping words and splitting them into even layers between two rows of teeth drunk with the repeated issuance of a promiscuous word, empty and vain, something borrowed from someone else, torso stiffly bent toward the dark ceiling, neck twisted into a rutting swan reeking of its own magnetic emanations, sniffing the bottom of his glass in search of the ultimate hostility, licking fingers, a face with the serenity of a bed of farmed oysters, left hand tracing semi-circles and broken loops in the air, unpreoccupied by the gangly grimaces of an audience already in the throes of whispering cursed tomorrows and then choking them back on their own saliva.

It was a major

and spasmodic chord that begat a new, considerable surge of
knowledge hitherto dumb and deadened. Before resuming fresh
jumbled and premonitory dreams, thinking of subterfuge, one
fitting sound that enables us to forget the roots of our tenacious
evil. Stomach cramps. Pangs. Puny coughs, sniffles, looks result-
ing from an indignant conscience. To form our wishes from
strange splatterings, wafting on the scent of burning wax.

VI

The Globalization of Poetry

Coimbra, 2001 — for Régis Bonvicino

Faces that outline a world
the rough draft of a calm and wise image
the unconscious physics of the streets
that separates noise from its nascent disturbance

some poets pose in front of neofascist
graffiti that mackle the walls
of the Faculdade de Ciências e Tecnologia
while others try to communicate with each other.

Cette phrase est en portugais
the incident that brings them together
makes the question yet more urgent
there where it's found and where it's not

VII

In the subsoil

for Elisabeth

of Covent Garden is found the Museum of Automata. In its collection there's a tiny room in which a sleeping woman's dream takes the shape of an enormous pale snake springing from a wardrobe under the terrified gaze of the man who shares her bed. The jaundiced cast of the latter foreshadows the great likelihood of approaching death. The furnishings themselves are characterized by their nondescript appearance, a most respectable and permanent and unremarkable arrangement. They represent the succor of a functional state in a universe thick with mystery — a life raft located smack dab in the middle of the gap between time and meaning.

There's a Kleenex box set on the night table. Sole concession to a modern metropolis's pop and swing, it prefigures a return to domestic hygiene after rubbing mucous membranes and the exchange of fluids. Disturbing weirdness of gears and levers that activate these low-tech marvels — they play an integral part of dream's slot machine.

Indivisible human creatures

overpowered by lurking and creeping inanity. Shouldn't the subject that is broached bring them back to what's essential? Remaining impermeable to the discourse that tries to seize it, making a virtue of mistakes, trying, moreover, to convince them of the constraints and merits of peristaltic aesthetics, from Gargantua's asswipe to Duchamp's urinal, the passing of Broodthaers's jellyfish and its sublime and indigestible beauty, not to mention Mona Hatoum's postmodern endoscopies, exploring the tiniest recesses of the Third Body, which, according to Valéry, can only attain unity in our soul.

Art's Childhood

Dante asks Giotto how he can bring to life such beautiful paint-
ings and engender such ugly children.

Besides

the art we call modern was born from the loss of a sense of the *je-ne-sais-quoi*, from the dubious dialectic of minimalism and maximalism, from fear and from the search for emptiness, from the desire to express pure essence, from death of the subject, from the symbolic reversibility of the anagram, from negative theology

Looking for the new Marcel

Duchamp in the gutter of the artistic *Who's Who*, sounding the depth of his hypertrophic indignation, very slowly becoming aware of the three sides of himself, musing about the most improbable ramifications of his synoptic evolution.

But this apparent

aporia of taste must not distract us from the essential need to affirm against the whole world the dialectical inclination of art considered from the viewpoint of production and consumption, which accounts for the interiorization and regurgitation of sound, image and sense.

Here

there's much fondness for the short, hard and mischievous word, for ineffectual and annoying aphorisms, for postcards and cream pies. You practice rag-tag aesthetics with your bad puns. You revel in the simple and democratic joys of objective surrealism.

Sometimes you like to imagine the contours and conjectural correspondence of scandal sheet poetry. Nevertheless, recent reports deny that anything supposedly revealed or transformed through language is a hoax

Without

indulging way too much in seriousness, would the feeling of belonging to a circle of friends and acquaintances sharing the same tastes, the same state of mind, would that constitute the last rampart against the degradation of meaning that results from the loss of the local validity of universal reading? One day, while drinking a couple Trappist beers, Ben asked me whether I knew why the hell we shared the same fascination for Satie, Joyce and Zappa. Was it to make sure that we had something to say to each other?

Exquisite Divan magnificent

Divan. Divine Divan. Divan Marquis de Sade. Divan stuffed with pathos. Sweet and sour Divan. Divan the Terrible. Divan so desirable. Late Divan graying in crepuscular light. Divan sofa Zappa-esque fart-artist with doily frills. Divan of delicate wicker unlaced sexy negligee. Joker Divan, waltzing with the confused clearness of stars, blathering about everything and nothing, dismissing passion and reason. Lugubrious and starless Divan.

To convert

our ideas into material things. To fight against the contradictions of a life subject to the whims of a stomach with the butterflies, an empty heart, a ruined liver. Such, it seems, is the calling of all the weird stuff in the world.

VIII

Will You Forgive Me?

I very much needed to surprise you, dive, climb and dive again in order to resurface despite my conscious flaws, to mine memories in search of some truthful witness, vicarious places, flunky middlemen (Joyce will return them to us in the saintultiplier). To observe without taking part. To reascend downpours. To shake up the universal. To transpose backgrounds and figures, like Arcimboldo and his cook-in-the-pan. To taste objects lacking in substance in every conceivable and imaginable way.

To darken

a few pages. To counterfeit contradictory vibrations with spasmophile writing. Fearing that our thoughts will be reduced to taking in only the immediate and illegible experience of the instant.

Will you tell me the meaning of

this beautiful disorder? And what of these words on which we unceasingly chomp and ruminate in order to avoid the hardship of a life far too infirm? What do we know, ultimately, of the supination of pleasures that sicken us while transporting us beyond the tolerable pneumatic limits of psychic disorder? The little we know must be spoken until the last tremor. The rest performed in the dignity of forgetfulness.

Probably

it's that inherent haste in mercenary passion that makes us concerned beings, of course, who nonetheless remain grateful for having been exposed to the confusion that governs the best moments of peristaltic consciousness.

That confusion, it amounts to a distinction for us.

Self-Portrait

I have the feeling that in observing me in that way he is
attempting to show me the way to a being who is on the verge
of leaving his own field of conscience, his own will multiplying
the gestures and movements that would enable him to savor hap-
piness or rather the satisfaction of feeling alive outside of any
hope for coherency

Yet this thought

haunts us with a growing conscience, redeemed by a fresh bout of intent. Intensity renewed through ritual execution. And through the violent expedient of the accident that fascinates so many of our contemporaries.

The art of living elsewhere.

IX

To abolish death

by accumulating things equivalent to the objective immensity of capital in place of the perception of eternity. We die from habit, finding refuge in leisure, in the style and passion of gigantic illuminated letters randomly drifting through our brains. Their message is simple, transparent. Meanwhile, we consent to the illusion that the living world itself becomes simply the effect of reduced vision. In the total clarity of those suburban insomniacs, we all speak the same language. A language that must never relieve us from the need to feel close to each other and expound on the unlikely and painful privilege of being driven by an inner life.

Invoking Joyce, Loyola, Sade, Broodthaers, Duchamp, Ponge, Warhol and other fetishist saints, not to speak of all those major petit-bourgeois writers who console us by demonstrating that the real revolution is one of language and that the word is no more than a pretext for reassembling whatever's missing from stabilizing our fundamental relation to being.

Nerves

are on edge. We're promised relief. We'd like to believe it, if only for an instant. If only to foil the snares of suggestion with double meanings. And rather than darken day, this invariable intent, this will to fight against the memory of intransitive offense. *We are what we thought we were.* And then this ensuing cold resignation emanating from darkness in order to attain a sweet provisional sleep, we want it sad and faithful.

Uninterrupted Slips and Setbacks

Unquiet strand of base pleasures miscarried on the steep menstrual slope of authorial arrogance. Time for a good tongue smack, your gaze rests on scraps sloth rejects or abandons. Interference detected by satellites usually presages a predictable dip.

Sky

darkens, someone lights a candle. Drape a heavy coat over your shoulders, dream of returning home and finding time to reflect on the consequences of a warm welcome back to normality.

quale [kwa-lay]: *Eng.* n 1. A property (such as hardness) considered apart from things that have that property. 2. A property that is experienced as distinct from any source it may have in a physical object. *Ital.* pron.a. 1. Which, what. 2. Who. 3. Some. 4. As, just as.

Made in the USA
Monee, IL
07 July 2026

56551140R00049